The Knights by Aristophanes

Translated from the Greek.

The reality is that little is known of Aristophanes actual life but eleven of his forty plays survive intact and upon those rest his deserved reputation as the Father of Comedy or, The Prince of Ancient Comedy.

Accounts agree that he was born sometime between 456BC and 446 BC. Many cities claim the honor of his birthplace and the most probable story makes him the son of Philippus of Ægina, and therefore only an adopted citizen of Athens, a distinction which, at times could be cruel, though he was raised and educated in Athens.

His plays are said to recreate the life of ancient Athens more realistically than any other author could. Intellectually his powers of ridicule were feared by his influential contemporaries; Plato himself singled out Aristophanes' play The Clouds as a slander that contributed to the trial and condemning to death of Socrates and although other satirical playwrights had also caricatured the philosopher his carried the most weight.

His now lost play, The Babylonians, was denounced by the demagogue Cleon as a slander against the Athenian polis. Aristophanes seems to have taken this criticism to heart and thereafter caricatured Cleon mercilessly in his subsequent plays, especially The Knights.

His life and playwriting years were undoubtedly long though again accounts as to the year of his death vary quite widely. What can be certain is that his legacy of surviving plays is in effect both a treasured legacy but also in itself the only surviving texts of Ancient Greek comedy.

Index of Contents

INTRODUCTION

This was the fourth play in order of time produced by Aristophanes on the Athenian stage; it was brought out at the Lenaean Festival, in January, 424 B.C. Of the author's previous efforts, two, 'The Revellers' and 'The Babylonians,' were apparently youthful essays, and are both lost. The other, 'The Acharnians,' forms the first of the three Comedies dealing directly with the War and its disastrous effects and urging the conclusion of Peace; for this reason it is better ranged along with its sequels, the 'Peace' and the 'Lysistrata,' and considered in conjunction with them.

In many respects 'The Knights' may be reckoned the great Comedian's masterpiece, the direct personal attack on the then all powerful Cleon, with its scathing satire and tremendous invective, being one of the most vigorous and startling things in literature. Already in 'The Acharnians' he had threatened to "cut up Cleon the Tanner into shoe-leather for the Knights," and he now proceeds to carry his menace into execution, "concentrating the whole force of his wit in the most unscrupulous and merciless fashion against his personal enemy." In the first-mentioned play Aristophanes had attacked and satirized the whole general policy of the democratic party—and incidentally Cleon, its leading spirit and mouthpiece since the death of Pericles; he had painted the miseries of war and invasion arising from this mistaken and mischievous line of action, as he regarded it, and had dwelt on the urgent necessity of peace in the interests of an exhausted country and ruined agriculture. Now he turns upon Cleon personally, and pays him back a hundredfold for the attacks the demagogue had made in the Public Assembly on the daring critic, and the abortive charge which the same unscrupulous enemy had brought against him in the Courts of having "slandered the city in the presence of foreigners." "In this bitterness of spirit the play stands in strong contrast with the good-humoured burlesque of 'The Acharnians' and the 'Peace,' or, indeed, with any other of the author's productions which has reached us."

The characters are five only. First and foremost comes Demos, 'The People,' typifying the Athenian democracy, a rich householder—a self-indulgent, superstitious, weak creature. He has had several overseers or factors in succession, to look after his estate and manage his slaves. The present one is known as 'the Paphlagonian,' or sometimes as 'the Tanner,' an unprincipled, lying, cheating, pilfering scoundrel, fawning and obsequious to his master, insolent towards his subordinates. Two of these are Nicias and Demosthenes. Here we have real names. Nicias was High Admiral of the Athenian navy at the time, and Demosthenes one of his Vice-Admirals; both held still more important commands later in connection with the Sicilian Expedition of 415-413 B.C. Fear of consequences apparently prevented the poet from doing the same in the case of Cleon, who is, of course, intended under the names of 'the Paphlagonian' and 'the Tanner.' Indeed, so great was the terror inspired by the great man that no artist was found bold enough to risk his powerful vengeance by caricaturing his features, and no actor dared to represent him on the stage. Aristophanes is said to have played the part himself, with his face, in the absence of a mask, smeared with wine-lees, roughly mimicking the purple and bloated visage of the demagogue. The remaining character is 'the Sausage-seller,' who is egged on by Nicias and Demosthenes to oust 'the Paphlagonian' from Demos' favour by outvying him in his own arts of impudent flattery, noisy boasting and unscrupulous allurement. After a fierce and stubbornly contested trial of wits and interchange of 'Billingsgate,' 'the Sausage-seller' beats his rival at his own weapons and gains his object; he supplants the disgraced favourite, who is driven out of the house with ignominy.

The Comedy takes its title, as was often the case, from the Chorus, which is composed of Knights—the order of citizens next to the highest at Athens, and embodying many of the old aristocratic preferences and prejudices.

The drama was adjudged the first prize—the 'Satyrs' of Cratinus being placed second—by acclamation, as such a masterpiece of wit and intrepidity certainly deserved to be; but, as usual, the political result was nil. The piece was applauded in the most enthusiastic manner, the satire on the sovereign multitude was forgiven, and—Cleon remained in as much favour as ever.

THE PERSONS

DEMOSTHENES.
NICIAS.
AGORACRITUS, a Sausage-seller.
CLEON.
DEMOS, an old man, typifying the Athenian people.
CHORUS OF KNIGHTS.

SCENE

In front of Demos' house at Athens.

THE KNIGHTS

DEMOSTHENES
Oh! alas! alas! Oh! woe! oh! woe! Miserable Paphlagonian! May the gods destroy both him and his cursed advice! Since that evil day when this new slave entered the house he has never ceased belabouring us with blows.

NICIAS
May the plague seize him, the arch-fiend—him and his lying tales!

DEMOSTHENES
Hah! my poor fellow, what is your condition?

NICIAS
Very wretched, just like your own.

DEMOSTHENES
Then come, let us sing a duet of groans in the style of Olympus.

DEMOSTHENES AND NICIAS
Boo, hoo! boo, hoo! boo, hoo! boo, hoo! boo, hoo! boo, hoo!!

DEMOSTHENES
Bah! 'tis lost labour to weep! Enough of groaning! Let us consider how to save our pelts.

NICIAS
But how to do it! Can you suggest anything?

DEMOSTHENES
Nay! you begin. I cede you the honour.

NICIAS
By Apollo! no, not I. Come, have courage! Speak, and then I will say what I think.

DEMOSTHENES
"Ah! would you but tell me what I should tell you!"

NICIAS
I dare not. How could I express my thoughts with the pomp of Euripides?

DEMOSTHENES
Oh! prithee, spare me! Do not pelt me with those vegetables, but find some way of leaving our master.

NICIAS
Well, then! Say "Let-us-bolt," like this, in one breath.

DEMOSTHENES
I follow you—"Let-us-bolt."

NICIAS
Now after "Let-us-bolt" say "at-top-speed!"

DEMOSTHENES
"At-top-speed!"

NICIAS
Splendid! Just as if you were masturbating yourself; first slowly, "Let-us-bolt"; then quick and firmly, "at-top-speed!"

DEMOSTHENES
Let-us-bolt, let-us-bolt-at-top-speed!

NICIAS
Hah! does that not please you?

DEMOSTHENES
I' faith, yes! yet I fear me your omen bodes no good to my hide.

NICIAS
How so?

DEMOSTHENES
Because hard rubbing abrades the skin when folk masturbate themselves.

NICIAS
The best thing we can do for the moment is to throw ourselves at the feet of the statue of some god.

DEMOSTHENES
Of which statue? Any statue? Do you then believe there are gods?

NICIAS
Certainly.

DEMOSTHENES
What proof have you?

NICIAS
The proof that they have taken a grudge against me. Is that not enough?

DEMOSTHENES
I'm convinced it is. But to pass on. Do you consent to my telling the spectators of our troubles?

NICIAS

'Twould not be amiss, and we might ask them to show us by their manner, whether our facts and actions are to their liking.

DEMOSTHENES
I will begin then. We have a very brutal master, a perfect glutton for beans, and most bad-tempered; 'tis Demos of the Pnyx, an intolerable old man and half deaf. The beginning of last month he bought a slave, a Paphlagonian tanner, an arrant rogue, the incarnation of calumny. This man of leather knows his old master thoroughly; he plays the fawning cur, flatters, cajoles; wheedles, and dupes him at will with little scraps of leavings, which he allows him to get. "Dear Demos," he will say, "try a single case and you will have done enough; then take your bath, eat, swallow and devour; here are three obols." Then the Paphlagonian filches from one of us what we have prepared and makes a present of it to our old man. T'other day I had just kneaded a Spartan cake at Pylos; the cunning rogue came behind my back, sneaked it and offered the cake, which was my invention, in his own name. He keeps us at a distance and suffers none but himself to wait upon the master; when Demos is dining, he keeps close to his side with a thong in his hand and puts the orators to flight. He keeps singing oracles to him, so that the old man now thinks of nothing but the Sibyl. Then, when he sees him thoroughly obfuscated, he uses all his cunning and piles up lies and calumnies against the household; then we are scourged and the Paphlagonian runs about among the slaves to demand contributions with threats and gathers 'em in with both hands. He will say, "You see how I have had Hylas beaten! Either content me or die at once!" We are forced to give, for else the old man tramples on us and makes us spew forth all our body contains. There must be an end to it, friend. Let us see! What can be done? Who will get us out of this mess?

NICIAS
The best thing, chum, is our famous "Let-us-bolt!"

DEMOSTHENES
But none can escape the Paphlagonian, his eye is everywhere. And what a stride! He has one leg on Pylos and the other in the Assembly; his rump is exactly over the land of the Chaonians, his hands are with the Aetolians and his mind with the Clopidians.

NICIAS
'Tis best then to die; but let us seek the most heroic death.

DEMOSTHENES
Let me bethink me, what is the most heroic?

NICIAS
Let us drink the blood of a bull; 'tis the death which Themistocles chose.

DEMOSTHENES
No, not that, but a bumper of good unmixed wine in honour of the Good Genius; perchance we may stumble on a happy thought.

NICIAS
Look at him! "Unmixed wine!" Your mind is on drink intent? Can a man strike out a brilliant thought when drunk?

DEMOSTHENES
Without question. Go, ninny, blow yourself out with water; do you dare to accuse wine of clouding the reason? Quote me more marvellous effects than those of wine. Look! when a man drinks, he is

rich, everything he touches succeeds, he gains lawsuits, is happy and helps his friends. Come, bring hither quick a flagon of wine, that I may soak my brain and get an ingenious idea.

NICIAS
Eh, my god! What can your drinking do to help us?

DEMOSTHENES
Much. But bring it to me, while I take my seat. Once drunk, I shall strew little ideas, little phrases, little reasonings everywhere.

NICIAS [Returning with a flagon]
It is lucky I was not caught in the house stealing the wine.

DEMOSTHENES
Tell me, what is the Paphlagonian doing now?

NICIAS
The wretch has just gobbled up some confiscated cakes; he is drunk and lies at full-length a-snoring on his hides.

DEMOSTHENES
Very well, come along, pour me out wine and plenty of it.

NICIAS
Take it and offer a libation to your Good Genius; taste, taste the liquor of the genial soil of Pramnium.

DEMOSTHENES
Oh, Good Genius! 'Tis thy will, not mine.

NICIAS
Prithee, tell me, what is it?

DEMOSTHENES
Run indoors quick and steal the oracles of the Paphlagonian, while he is asleep.

NICIAS
Bless me! I fear this Good Genius will be but a very Bad Genius for me.

DEMOSTHENES
And set the flagon near me, that I may moisten my wit to invent some brilliant notion.

NICIAS [Enters the house and returns at once]
How the Paphlagonian grunts and snores! I was able to seize the sacred oracle, which he was guarding with the greatest care, without his seeing me.

DEMOSTHENES
Oh! clever fellow! Hand it here, that I may read. Come, pour me out some drink, bestir yourself! Let me see what there is in it. Oh! prophecy! Some drink! some drink! Quick!

NICIAS

Well! what says the oracle?

DEMOSTHENES
Pour again.

NICIAS
Is "pour again" in the oracle?

DEMOSTHENES
Oh, Bacis!

NICIAS
But what is in it?

DEMOSTHENES
Quick! some drink!

NICIAS
Bacis is very dry!

DEMOSTHENES
Oh! miserable Paphlagonian! This then is why you have so long taken such precautions; your horoscope gave you qualms of terror.

NICIAS
What does it say?

DEMOSTHENES
It says here how he must end.

NICIAS
And how?

DEMOSTHENES
How? the oracle announces clearly that a dealer in oakum must first govern the city.

NICIAS
First dealer. And after him, who?

DEMOSTHENES
After him, a sheep-dealer.

NICIAS
Two dealers, eh? And what is this one's fate?

DEMOSTHENES
To reign until a greater scoundrel than he arises; then he perishes and in his place the leather-seller appears, the Paphlagonian robber, the bawler, who roars like a torrent.

NICIAS
And the leather-seller must destroy the sheep-seller?

DEMOSTHENES
Yes.

NICIAS
Oh! woe is me! Where can another seller be found, is there ever a one left?

DEMOSTHENES
There is yet one, who plies a firstrate trade.

NICIAS
Tell me, pray, what is that?

DEMOSTHENES
You really want to know?

NICIAS
Yes.

DEMOSTHENES
Well then! 'tis a sausage-seller who must overthrow him.

NICIAS
A sausage-seller! Ah! by Posidon! what a fine trade! But where can this man be found?

DEMOSTHENES
Let us seek him.

NICIAS
Lo! there he is, going towards the market-place; 'tis the gods, the gods who send him!

DEMOSTHENES
This way, this way, oh, lucky sausage-seller, come forward, dear friend, our saviour, the saviour of our city.

SAUSAGE-SELLER
What is it? Why do you call me?

DEMOSTHENES
Come here, come and learn about your good luck, you who are Fortune's favourite!

NICIAS
Come! Relieve him of his basket-tray and tell him the oracle of the god; I will go and look after the Paphlagonian.

DEMOSTHENES
First put down all your gear, then worship the earth and the gods.

SAUSAGE-SELLER
'Tis done. What is the matter?

DEMOSTHENES
Happiness, riches, power; to-day you have nothing, to-morrow you will have all, oh! chief of happy Athens.

SAUSAGE-SELLER
Why not leave me to wash my tripe and to sell my sausages instead of making game of me?

DEMOSTHENES
Oh! the fool! Your tripe! Do you see these tiers of people?

SAUSAGE-SELLER
Yes.

DEMOSTHENES
You shall be master to them all, governor of the market, of the harbours, of the Pnyx; you shall trample the Senate under foot, be able to cashier the generals, load them with fetters, throw them into gaol, and you will play the debauchee in the Prytaneum.

SAUSAGE-SELLER
What! I?

DEMOSTHENES
You, without a doubt. But you do not yet see all the glory awaiting you. Stand on your basket and look at all the islands that surround Athens.

SAUSAGE-SELLER
I see them. What then?

DEMOSTHENES
Look at the storehouses and the shipping.

SAUSAGE-SELLER
Yes, I am looking.

DEMOSTHENES
Exists there a mortal more blest than you? Furthermore, turn your right eye towards Caria and your left towards Chalcedon.

SAUSAGE-SELLER
'Tis then a blessing to squint!

DEMOSTHENES
No, but 'tis you who are going to trade away all this. According to the oracle you must become the greatest of men.

SAUSAGE-SELLER
Just tell me how a sausage-seller can become a great man.

DEMOSTHENES
That is precisely why you will be great, because you are a sad rascal without shame, no better than a common market rogue.

SAUSAGE-SELLER
I do not hold myself worthy of wielding power.

DEMOSTHENES
Oh! by the gods! Why do you not hold yourself worthy? Have you then such a good opinion of yourself? Come, are you of honest parentage?

SAUSAGE-SELLER
By the gods! No! of very bad indeed.

DEMOSTHENES
Spoilt child of fortune, everything fits together to ensure your greatness.

SAUSAGE-SELLER
But I have not had the least education. I can only read, and that very badly.

DEMOSTHENES
That is what may stand in your way, almost knowing how to read. The demagogues will neither have an educated nor an honest man; they require an ignoramus and a rogue. But do not, do not let go this gift, which the oracle promises.

SAUSAGE-SELLER
But what does the oracle say?

DEMOSTHENES
Faith! it is put together in very fine enigmatical style, as elegant as it is clear: "When the eagle-tanner with the hooked claws shall seize a stupid dragon, a blood-sucker, it will be an end to the hot Paphlagonian pickled garlic. The god grants great glory to the sausage-sellers unless they prefer to sell their wares."

SAUSAGE-SELLER
In what way does this concern me? Pray instruct my ignorance.

DEMOSTHENES
The eagle-tanner is the Paphlagonian.

SAUSAGE-SELLER
What do the hooked claws mean?

DEMOSTHENES
It means to say, that he robs and pillages us with his claw-like hands.

SAUSAGE-SELLER
And the dragon?

DEMOSTHENES
That is quite clear. The dragon is long and so also is the sausage; the sausage like the dragon is a drinker of blood. Therefore the oracle says, that the dragon will triumph over the eagle-tanner, if he does not let himself be cajoled with words.

SAUSAGE-SELLER
The oracles of the gods summon me! Faith! I do not at all understand how I can be capable of governing the people.

DEMOSTHENES
Nothing simpler. Continue your trade. Mix and knead together all the state business as you do for your sausages. To win the people, always cook them some savoury that pleases them. Besides, you possess all the attributes of a demagogue; a screeching, horrible voice, a perverse, cross-grained nature and the language of the market-place. In you all is united which is needful for governing. The oracles are in your favour, even including that of Delphi. Come, take a chaplet, offer a libation to the god of Stupidity and take care to fight vigorously.

SAUSAGE-SELLER
Who will be my ally? for the rich fear the Paphlagonian and the poor shudder at the sight of him.

DEMOSTHENES
You will have a thousand brave Knights, who detest him, on your side; also the honest citizens amongst the spectators, those who are men of brave hearts, and finally myself and the god. Fear not, you will not see his features, for none have dared to make a mask resembling him. But the public have wit enough to recognize him.

NICIAS
Oh! mercy! here is the Paphlagonian!

CLEON
By the twelve gods! Woe betide you, who have too long been conspiring against Demos. What means this Chalcidian cup? No doubt you are provoking the Chalcidians to revolt. You shall be killed, butchered, you brace of rogues.

DEMOSTHENES
What! are you for running away? Come, come, stand firm, bold Sausage-seller, do not betray us. To the rescue, oh! Knights. Now is the time. Simon, Panaetius, get you to the right wing; they are coming on; hold tight and return to the charge. I can see the dust of their horses' hoofs; they are galloping to our aid. Courage! Repel, attack them, put them to flight.

CHORUS
Strike, strike the villain, who has spread confusion amongst the ranks of the Knights, this public robber, this yawning gulf of plunder, this devouring Charybdis, this villain, this villain, this villain! I cannot say the word too often, for he is a villain a thousand times a day. Come, strike, drive, hurl him over and crush him to pieces; hate him as we hate him; stun him with your blows and your shouts. And beware lest he escape you; he knows the way Eucrates took straight to a bran sack for concealment.

CLEON
Oh! veteran Heliasts, brotherhood of the three obols, whom I fostered by bawling at random, help me; I am being beaten to death by rebels.

CHORUS
And 'tis justice; you devour the public funds that all should share in; you treat the officers answerable for the revenue like the fruit of the fig tree, squeezing them to find which are still green or more or less ripe; and, when you find one simple and timid, you force him to come from the

Chersonese, then you seize him by the middle, throttle him by the neck, while you twist his shoulder back; he falls and you devour him. Besides, you know very well how to select from among the citizens those who are as meek as lambs, rich, without guile and loathers of lawsuits.

CLEON
Eh! what! Knights, are you helping them? But, if I am beaten, 'tis in your cause, for I was going to propose to erect you a statue in the city in memory of your bravery.

CHORUS
Oh! the impostor! the dull varlet! See! he treats us like old dotards and crawls at our feet to deceive us; but the cunning wherein lies his power shall this time recoil on himself; he trips up himself by resorting to such artifices.

CLEON
Oh Citizens! oh people! see how these brutes are bursting my belly.

CHORUS
What shouts! but 'tis this very bawling that incessantly upsets the city!

SAUSAGE-SELLER
I can shout too—and so loud that you will flee with fear.

CHORUS
If you shout louder than he does, I will strike up the triumphal hymn; if you surpass him in impudence, the cake is ours.

CLEON
I denounce this fellow; he has had tasty stews exported from Athens for the Spartan fleet.

SAUSAGE-SELLER
And I denounce him, who runs into the Prytaneum with empty belly and comes out with it full.

DEMOSTHENES
And by Zeus! he carries off bread, meat, and fish, which is forbidden. Pericles himself never had this right.

CLEON
You are travelling the right road to get killed.

SAUSAGE-SELLER
I'll bawl three times as loud as you.

CLEON
I will deafen you with my yells.

SAUSAGE-SELLER
And I you with my bellowing.

CLEON
I shall calumniate you, if you become a Strategus.

SAUSAGE-SELLER
Dog, I will lay your back open with the lash.

CLEON
I will make you drop your arrogance.

SAUSAGE-SELLER
I will baffle your machinations.

CLEON
Dare to look me in the face!

SAUSAGE-SELLER
I too was brought up in the market-place.

CLEON
I will cut you to shreds if you whisper a word.

SAUSAGE-SELLER
I will daub you with dung if you open your mouth.

CLEON
I own I am a thief; do you admit yourself another.

SAUSAGE-SELLER
By our Hermes of the market-place, if caught in the act, why, I perjure myself before those who saw me.

CLEON
These are my own special tricks. I will denounce you to the Prytanes as the owner of sacred tripe, that has not paid tithe.

CHORUS
Oh! you scoundrel! you impudent bawler! everything is filled with your daring, all Attica, the Assembly, the Treasury, the decrees, the tribunals. As a furious torrent you have overthrown our city; your outcries have deafened Athens and, posted upon a high rock, you have lain in wait for the tribute moneys as the fisherman does for the tunny-fish.

CLEON
I know your tricks; 'tis an old plot resoled.

SAUSAGE-SELLER
If you know naught of soling, I understand nothing of sausages; you, who cut bad leather on the slant to make it look stout and deceive the country yokels. They had not worn it a day before it had stretched some two spans.

DEMOSTHENES
'Tis the very trick he served me; both my neighbours and my friends laughed heartily at me, and before I reached Pergasae I was swimming in my shoes.

CHORUS

Have you not always shown that blatant impudence, which is the sole strength of our orators? You push it so far, that you, the head of the State, dare to milk the purses of the opulent aliens and, at sight of you, the son of Hippodamus melts into tears. But here is another man, who gives me pleasure, for he is a much greater rascal than you; he will overthrow you; 'tis easy to see, that he will beat you in roguery, in brazenness and in clever turns. Come, you, who have been brought up among the class which to-day gives us all our great men, show us that a liberal education is mere tomfoolery.

SAUSAGE-SELLER
Just hear what sort of fellow that fine citizen is.

CLEON
Will you not let me speak?

SAUSAGE-SELLER
Assuredly not, for I also am a sad rascal.

CHORUS
If he does not give in at that, tell him your parents were sad rascals too.

CLEON
Once more, will you not let me speak?

SAUSAGE-SELLER
No, by Zeus!

CLEON
Yes, by Zeus, but you shall!

SAUSAGE-SELLER
No, by Posidon! We will fight first to see who shall speak first.

CLEON
I will die sooner.

SAUSAGE-SELLER
I will not let you....

CHORUS
Let him, in the name of the gods, let him die.

CLEON
What makes you so bold as to dare to speak to my face?

SAUSAGE-SELLER
'Tis that I know both how to speak and how to cook.

CLEON
Hah! the fine speaker! Truly, if some business matter fell your way, you would know thoroughly well how to attack it, to carve it up alive! Shall I tell you what has happened to you? Like so many others, you have gained some petty lawsuit against some alien. Did you drink enough water to inspire you?

Did you mutter over the thing sufficiently through the night, spout it along the street, recite it to all you met? Have you bored your friends enough with it? 'Tis then for this you deem yourself an orator. Ah! poor fool!

SAUSAGE-SELLER
And what do you drink yourself then, to be able all alone by yourself to dumbfound and stupefy the city so with your clamour?

CLEON
Can you match me with a rival? Me! When I have devoured a good hot tunny-fish and drunk on top of it a great jar of unmixed wine, I hold up the Generals of Pylos to public scorn.

SAUSAGE-SELLER
And I, when I have bolted the tripe of an ox together with a sow's belly and swallowed the broth as well, I am fit, though slobbering with grease, to bellow louder than all orators and to terrify Nicias.

CHORUS
I admire your language so much; the only thing I do not approve is that you swallow all the broth yourself.

CLEON
E'en though you gorged yourself on sea-dogs, you would not beat the Milesians.

SAUSAGE-SELLER
Give me a bullock's breast to devour, and I am a man to traffic in mines.

CLEON
I will rush into the Senate and set them all by the ears.

SAUSAGE-SELLER
And I will lug out your gut to stuff like a sausage.

CLEON
As for me, I will seize you by the rump and hurl you head foremost through the door.

CHORUS
In any case, by Posidon, 'twill only be when you have thrown me there first.

CLEON
Beware of the carcan!

SAUSAGE-SELLER
I denounce you for cowardice.

CLEON
I will tan your hide.

SAUSAGE-SELLER
I will flay you and make a thief's pouch with the skin.

CLEON

I will peg you out on the ground.

SAUSAGE-SELLER
I will slice you into mince-meat.

CLEON
I will tear out your eyelashes.

SAUSAGE-SELLER
I will slit your gullet.

DEMOSTHENES
We will set his mouth open with a wooden stick as the cooks do with pigs; we will tear out his tongue, and, looking down his gaping throat, will see whether his inside has any pimples.

CHORUS
Thus then at Athens we have something more fiery than fire, more impudent than impudence itself! 'Tis a grave matter; come, we will push and jostle him without mercy. There, you grip him tightly under the arms; if he gives way at the onset, you will find him nothing but a craven; I know my man.

SAUSAGE-SELLER
That he has been all his life and he has only made himself a name by reaping another's harvest; and now he has tied up the ears he gathered over there, he lets them dry and seeks to sell them.

CLEON
I do not fear you as long as there is a Senate and a people which stands like a fool, gaping in the air.

CHORUS
What unparalleled impudence! 'Tis ever the same brazen front. If I don't hate you, why, I'm ready to take the place of the one blanket Cratinus wets; I'll offer to play a tragedy by Morsimus. Oh! You cheat! who turn all into money, who flutter from one extortion to another; may you disgorge as quickly as you have crammed yourself! Then only would I sing, "Let us drink, let us drink to this happy event!" Then even the son of Iulius, the old niggard, would empty his cup with transports of joy, crying, "Io, Paean! Io, Bacchus!"

CLEON
By Posidon! You! would you beat me in impudence! If you succeed, may I no longer have my share of the victims offered to Zeus on the city altar.

SAUSAGE-SELLER
And I, I swear by the blows that have so oft rained upon my shoulders since infancy, and by the knives that have cut me, that I will show more effrontery than you; as sure as I have rounded this fine stomach by feeding on the pieces of bread that had cleansed other folk's greasy fingers.

CLEON
On pieces of bread, like a dog! Ah! wretch! you have the nature of a dog and you dare to fight a cynecephalus?

SAUSAGE-SELLER

I have many another trick in my sack, memories of my childhood's days. I used to linger around the cooks and say to them, "Look, friends, don't you see a swallow? 'tis the herald of springtime." And while they stood, their noses in the air, I made off with a piece of meat.

CHORUS
Oh! most clever man! How well thought out! You did as the eaters of artichokes, you gathered them before the return of the swallows.

SAUSAGE-SELLER
They could make nothing of it; or, if they suspected a trick, I hid the meat in my breeches and denied the thing by all the gods; so that an orator, seeing me at the game, cried, "This child will get on; he has the mettle that makes a statesman."

CHORUS
He argued rightly; to steal, perjure yourself and make a receiver of your rump are three essentials for climbing high.

CLEON
I will stop your insolence, or rather the insolence of both of you. I will throw myself upon you like a terrible hurricane ravaging both land and sea at the will of its fury.

SAUSAGE-SELLER
Then I will gather up my sausages and entrust myself to the kindly waves of fortune so as to make you all the more enraged.

DEMOSTHENES
And I will watch in the bilges in case the boat should make water.

CLEON
No, by Demeter! I swear, 'twill not be with impunity that you have thieved so many talents from the Athenians.

CHORUS [To the **SAUSAGE-SELLER**]
Oh! oh! reef your sail a bit! Here is Boreas blowing calumniously.

CLEON
I know that you got ten talents out of Potidaea.

SAUSAGE-SELLER
Hold! I will give you one; but keep it dark!

CHORUS
Hah! that will please him mightily; now you can travel under full sail.

SAUSAGE-SELLER
Yes, the wind has lost its violence.

CLEON
I will bring four suits against you, each of one hundred talents.

SAUSAGE-SELLER

And I twenty against you for shirking duty and more than a thousand for robbery.

CLEON
I maintain that your parents were guilty of sacrilege against the goddess.

SAUSAGE-SELLER
And I, that one of your grandfathers was a satellite....

CLEON
To whom? Explain!

SAUSAGE-SELLER
To Byrsina, the mother of Hippias.

CLEON
You are an impostor.

SAUSAGE-SELLER
And you are a rogue.

CHORUS
Hit him hard.

CLEON
Oh, oh, dear! The conspirators are murdering me!

CHORUS
Strike, strike with all your might; bruise his belly, lashing him with your guts and your tripe; punish him with both arms! Oh! Vigorous assailant and intrepid heart! Have you not routed him totally in this duel of abuse? how shall I give tongue to my joy and sufficiently praise you?

CLEON
Ah! by Demeter! I was not ignorant of this plot against me; I knew it was forming, that the chariot of war was being put together.

CHORUS [To **SAUSAGE-SELLER**]
Look out, look out! Come, outfence him with some wheelwright slang?

SAUSAGE-SELLER
His tricks at Argos do not escape me. Under pretence of forming an alliance with the Argives, he is hatching a plot with the Lacedaemonians there; and I know why the bellows are blowing and the metal that is on the anvil; 'tis the question of the prisoners.

CHORUS
Well done! Forge on, if he be a wheelwright.

SAUSAGE-SELLER
And there are men at Sparta who are hammering the iron with you; but neither gold nor silver nor prayers nor anything else shall impede my denouncing your trickery to the Athenians.

CLEON

As for me, I hasten to the Senate to reveal your plotting, your nightly gatherings in the city, your trafficking with the Medes and with the Great King, and all you are foraging for in Boeotia.

SAUSAGE-SELLER
What price then is paid for forage by Boeotians?

CLEON
Oh! by Heracles! I will tan your hide.

CHORUS
Come, if you have both wit and heart, now is the time to show it, as on the day when you hid the meat in your breeches, as you say. Hasten to the Senate, for he will rush there like a tornado to calumniate us all and give vent to his fearful bellowings.

SAUSAGE-SELLER
I am going, but first I must rid myself of my tripe and my knives; I will leave them here.

CHORUS
Stay! rub your neck with lard; in this way you will slip between the fingers of calumny.

SAUSAGE-SELLER
Spoken like a finished master of fence.

CHORUS
Now, bolt down these cloves of garlic.

SAUSAGE-SELLER
Pray, what for?

CHORUS
Well primed with garlic, you will have greater mettle for the fight. But hurry, hurry, bestir yourself!

SAUSAGE-SELLER
That's just what I am doing.

CHORUS
And, above all, bite your foe, rend him to atoms, tear off his comb and do not return until you have devoured his wattles. Go! Make your attack with a light heart, avenge me and may Zeus guard you! I burn to see you return the victor and laden with chaplets of glory. And you, spectators, enlightened critics of all kinds of poetry, lend an ear to my anapaests.

CHORUS
Had one of the old authors asked to mount this stage to recite his verses, he would not have found it hard to persuade me. But our poet of to-day is likewise worthy of this favour; he shares our hatred, he dares to tell the truth, he boldly braves both waterspouts and hurricanes. Many among you, he tells us, have expressed wonder, that he has not long since had a piece presented in his own name, and have asked the reason why. This is what he bids us say in reply to your questions; 'tis not without grounds that he has courted the shade, for, in his opinion, nothing is more difficult than to cultivate the comic Muse; many court her, but very few secure her favours. Moreover, he knows that you are fickle by nature and betray your poets when they grow old. What fate befell Magnes,

when his hair went white? Often enough has he triumphed over his rivals; he has sung in all keys, played the lyre and fluttered wings; he turned into a Lydian and even into a gnat, daubed himself with green to become a frog. All in vain! When young, you applauded him; in his old age you hooted and mocked him, because his genius for raillery had gone. Cratinus again was like a torrent of glory rushing across the plain, uprooting oak, plane tree and rivals and bearing them pell-mell in its wake. The only songs at the banquet were, 'Doro, shod with lying tales' and 'Adepts of the Lyric Muse'; so great was his renown. Look at him now! he drivels, his lyre has neither strings nor keys, his voice quivers, but you have no pity for him, and you let him wander about as he can, like Connas, his temples circled with a withered chaplet; the poor old fellow is dying of thirst; he who, in honour of his glorious past, should be in the Prytaneum drinking at his ease, and instead of trudging the country should be sitting amongst the first row of the spectators, close to the statue of Dionysus and loaded with perfumes. Crates, again, have you done hounding him with your rage and your hisses? True, 'twas but meagre fare that his sterile Muse could offer you; a few ingenious fancies formed the sole ingredients, but nevertheless he knew how to stand firm and to recover from his falls. 'Tis such examples that frighten our poet; in addition, he would tell himself, that before being a pilot, he must first know how to row, then to keep watch at the prow, after that how to gauge the winds, and that only then would he be able to command his vessel. If then you approve this wise caution and his resolve that he would not bore you with foolish nonsense, raise loud waves of applause in his favour this day, so that, at this Lenaean feast, the breath of your favour may swell the sails of his trumphant galley and the poet may withdraw proud of his success, with head erect and his face beaming with delight.

Posidon, god of the racing steed, I salute you, you who delight in their neighing and in the resounding clatter of their brass-shod hoofs, god of the swift galleys, which, loaded with mercenaries, cleave the seas with their azure beaks, god of the equestrian contests, in which young rivals, eager for glory, ruin themselves for the sake of distinction with their chariots in the arena, come and direct our chorus; Posidon with the trident of gold, you, who reign over the dolphins, who are worshipped at Sunium and at Geraestus beloved of Phormio, and dear to the whole city above all the immortals, I salute you!

Let us sing the glory of our forefathers; ever victors, both on land and sea, they merit that Athens, rendered famous by these, her worthy sons, should write their deeds upon the sacred peplus. As soon as they saw the enemy, they at once sprang at him without ever counting his strength. Should one of them fall in the conflict, he would shake off the dust, deny his mishap and begin the struggle anew. Not one of these Generals of old time would have asked Cleaenetus to be fed at the cost of the state; but our present men refuse to fight, unless they get the honours of the Prytaneum and precedence in their seats. As for us, we place our valour gratuitously at the service of Athens and of her gods; our only hope is, that, should peace ever put a term to our toils, you will not grudge us our long, scented hair nor our delicate care for our toilet.

Oh! Pallas, guardian of Athens, you, who reign over the most pious city, the most powerful, the richest in warriors and in poets, hasten to my call, bringing in your train our faithful ally in all our expeditions and combats, Victory, who smiles on our choruses and fights with us against our rivals. Oh! goddess! manifest yourself to our sight; this day more than ever we deserve that you should ensure our triumph.

We will sing likewise the exploits of our steeds! they are worthy of our praises; in what invasions, what fights have I not seen them helping us! But especially admirable were they, when they bravely leapt upon the galleys, taking nothing with them but a coarse wine, some cloves of garlic and onions; despite this, they nevertheless seized the sweeps just like men, curved their backs over the thwarts and shouted, "Hippopopoh! Give way! Come, all pull together! Come, come! How! Samphoras! Are you not rowing?" They rushed down upon the coast of Corinth, and the youngest hollowed out beds in the sand with their hoofs or went to fetch coverings; instead of luzern, they had no food but crabs, which they caught on the strand and even in the sea; so that Theorus causes a Corinthian crab to say, "'Tis a cruel fate, oh Posidon! neither my deep hiding-places, whether on land or at sea, can help me to escape the Knights."

Welcome, oh, dearest and bravest of men! How distracted I have been during your absence! But here you are back, safe and sound. Tell us about the fight you have had.

SAUSAGE-SELLER
The important thing is that I have beaten the Senate.

CHORUS
All glory to you! Let us burst into shouts of joy! You speak well, but your deeds are even better. Come, tell me everything in detail; what a long journey would I not be ready to take to hear your tale! Come, dear friend, speak with full confidence to your admirers.

SAUSAGE-SELLER
The story is worth hearing. Listen! From here I rushed straight to the Senate, right in the track of this man; he was already letting loose the storm, unchaining the lightning, crushing the Knights beneath huge mountains of calumnies heaped together and having all the air of truth; he called you conspirators and his lies caught root like weeds in every mind; dark were the looks on every side and brows were knitted. When I saw that the Senate listened to him favourably and was being tricked by his imposture, I said to myself, "Come, gods of rascals and braggarts, gods of all fools, toad-eaters and braggarts and thou, market-place, where I was bred from my earliest days, give me unbridled audacity, an untiring chatter and a shameless voice." No sooner had I ended this prayer than a lewd man broke wind on my right. "Hah! 'tis a good omen," said I, and prostrated myself; then I burst open the door by a vigorous push with my back, and, opening my mouth to the utmost, shouted, "Senators, I wanted you to be the first to hear the good news; since the War broke out, I have never seen anchovies at a lower price!" All faces brightened at once and I was voted a chaplet for my good tidings; and I added, "With a couple of words I will reveal to you, how you can have quantities of anchovies for an obol; 'tis to seize on all the dishes the merchants have." With mouths gaping with admiration, they applauded me. However, the Paphlagonian winded the matter and, well knowing the sort of language which pleases the Senate best, said, "Friends, I am resolved to offer one hundred oxen to the goddess in recognition of this happy event." The Senate at once veered to his side. So when I saw myself defeated by this ox filth, I outbade the fellow, crying, "Two hundred!" And beyond this I moved, that a vow be made to Diana of a thousand goats if the next day anchovies should only be worth an obol a hundred. And the Senate looked towards me again. The other, stunned with the blow, grew delirious in his speech, and at last the Prytanes and the guards dragged him out. The Senators then stood talking noisily about the anchovies. Cleon, however, begged them to listen to the Lacedaemonian envoy, who had come to make proposals of peace; but all with one accord, cried, "'Tis certainly not the moment to think of peace now! If anchovies are so cheap, what need have we of peace? Let the war take its course!" And with loud shouts they demanded that the Prytanes should close the sitting and then leapt over the rails in all directions. As for me, I slipped away to buy all the coriander seed and leeks there were on the market and gave it to them gratis as seasoning for their anchovies. 'Twas marvellous! They loaded me with praises and caresses; thus I conquered the Senate with an obol's worth of leeks, and here I am.

CHORUS

Bravo! you are the spoilt child of Fortune. Ah! our knave has found his match in another, who has far better tricks in his sack, a thousand kinds of knaveries and of wily words. But the fight begins afresh; take care not to weaken; you know that I have long been your most faithful ally.

SAUSAGE-SELLER
Ah! ah! here comes the Paphlagonian! One would say, 'twas a hurricane lashing the sea and rolling the waves before it in its fury. He looks as if he wanted to swallow me up alive! Ye gods! what an impudent knave!

CLEON
To my aid, my beloved lies! I am going to destroy you, or my name is lost.

SAUSAGE-SELLER
Oh! how he diverts me with his threats! His bluster makes me laugh! And I dance the mothon for joy, and sing at the top of my voice, cuckoo!

CLEON
Ah! by Demeter! if I do not kill and devour you, may I die!

SAUSAGE-SELLER
If you do not devour me? and I, if I do not drink your blood to the last drop, and then burst with indigestion.

CLEON
I, I will strangle you, I swear it by the precedence which Pylos gained me.

SAUSAGE-SELLER
By the precedence! Ah! might I see you fall from your precedence into the hindmost seat!

CLEON
By heaven! I will put you to the torture.

SAUSAGE-SELLER
What a lively wit! Come, what's the best to give you to eat? What do you prefer? A purse?

CLEON
I will tear out your inside with my nails.

SAUSAGE-SELLER
And I will cut off your victuals at the Prytaneum.

CLEON
I will haul you before Demos, who will mete out justice to you.

SAUSAGE-SELLER
And I too will drag you before him and belch forth more calumnies than you.

CLEON
Why, poor fool, he does not believe you, whereas I play with him at will.

SAUSAGE-SELLER

So that Demos is your property, your contemptible creature.

CLEON
'Tis because I know the dishes that please him.

SAUSAGE-SELLER
And these are little mouthfuls, which you serve to him like a clever nurse. You chew the pieces and place some in small quantities in his mouth, while you swallow three parts yourself.

CLEON
Thanks to my skill, I know exactly how to enlarge or contract this gullet.

SAUSAGE-SELLER
I can do as much with my rump.

CLEON
Hah! my friend, you tricked me at the Senate, but have a care! Let us go before Demos.

SAUSAGE-SELLER
That's easily done; come, let's along without delay.

CLEON
Oh, Demos! Come, I adjure you to help me, my father!

SAUSAGE-SELLER
Come, oh, my dear little Demos; come and see how I am insulted.

DEMOS
What a hubbub! To the Devil with you, bawlers! alas! my olive branch, which they have torn down! Ah! 'tis you, Paphlagonian. And who, pray, has been maltreating you?

CLEON
You are the cause of this man and these young people having covered me with blows.

DEMOS
And why?

CLEON
Because you love me passionately, Demos.

DEMOS
And you, who are you?

SAUSAGE-SELLER
His rival. For many a long year have I loved you, have I wished to do you honour, I and a crowd of other men of means. But this rascal here has prevented us. You resemble those young men who do not know where to choose their lovers; you repulse honest folk; to earn your favours, one has to be a lamp-seller, a cobbler, a tanner or a currier.

CLEON
I am the benefactor of the people.

SAUSAGE-SELLER
In what way, an it please you?

CLEON
In what way? I supplanted the Generals at Pylos, I hurried thither and I brought back the Laconian captives.

SAUSAGE-SELLER
And I, whilst simply loitering, cleared off with a pot from a shop, which another fellow had been boiling.

CLEON
Demos, convene the assembly at once to decide which of us two loves you best and most merits your favour.

SAUSAGE-SELLER
Yes, yes, provided it be not at the Pnyx.

DEMOS
I could not sit elsewhere; 'tis at the Pnyx, that you must appear before me.

SAUSAGE-SELLER
Ah! great gods! I am undone! At home this old fellow is the most sensible of men, but the instant he is seated on those cursed stone seats, he is there with mouth agape as if he were hanging up figs by their stems to dry.

CHORUS
Come, loose all sail. Be bold, skilful in attack and entangle him in arguments which admit of no reply. It is difficult to beat him, for he is full of craft and pulls himself out of the worst corners. Collect all your forces to come forth from this fight covered with glory, but take care! Let him not assume the attack, get ready your grapples and advance with your vessel to board him!

CLEON
Oh! guardian goddess of our city! oh! Athené! if it be true that next to Lysicles, Cynna and Salabaccha none have done so much good for the Athenian people as I, suffer me to continue to be fed at the Prytaneum without working; but if I hate you, if I am not ready to fight in your defence alone and against all, may I perish, be sawn to bits alive and my skin be cut up into thongs.

SAUSAGE-SELLER
And I, Demos, if it be not true, that I love and cherish you, may I be cooked in a stew; and if that is not saying enough, may I be grated on this table with some cheese and then hashed, may a hook be passed through my testicles and let me be dragged thus to the Ceramicus!

CLEON
Is it possible, Demos, to love you more than I do? And firstly, as long as you have governed with my consent, have I not filled your treasury, putting pressure on some, torturing others or begging of them, indifferent to the opinion of private individuals, and solely anxious to please you?

SAUSAGE-SELLER

There is nothing so wonderful in all that, Demos; I will do as much; I will thieve the bread of others to serve up to you. No, he has neither love for you nor kindly feeling; his only care is to warm himself with your wood, and I will prove it. You, who, sword in hand, saved Attica from the Median yoke at Marathon; you, whose glorious triumphs we love to extol unceasingly, look, he cares little whether he sees you seated uncomfortably upon a stone; whereas I, I bring you this cushion, which I have sewn with my own hands. Rise and try this nice soft seat. Did you not put enough strain on your breeches at Salamis?

DEMOS
Who are you then? Can you be of the race of Harmodius? Upon my faith, 'tis nobly done and like a true friend of Demos.

CLEON
Petty flattery to prove him your goodwill!

SAUSAGE-SELLER
But you have caught him with even smaller baits!

CLEON
Never had Demos a defender or a friend more devoted than myself; on my head, on my life, I swear it!

SAUSAGE-SELLER
You pretend to love him and for eight years you have seen him housed in casks, in crevices and dovecots, where he is blinded with the smoke, and you lock him in without pity; Archeptolemus brought peace and you tore it to ribbons; the envoys who come to propose a truce you drive from the city with kicks in their backsides.

CLEON
This is that Demos may rule over all the Greeks; for the oracles predict that, if he is patient, he must one day sit as judge in Arcadia at five obols per day. Meanwhile, I will nourish him, look after him and, above all, I will ensure to him his three obols.

SAUSAGE-SELLER
No, little you care for his reigning in Arcadia, 'tis to pillage and impose on the allies at will that you reckon; you wish the War to conceal your rogueries as in a mist, that Demos may see nothing of them, and harassed by cares, may only depend on yourself for his bread. But if ever peace is restored to him, if ever he returns to his lands to comfort himself once more with good cakes, to greet his cherished olives, he will know the blessings you have kept him out of, even though paying him a salary; and, filled with hatred and rage, he will rise, burning with desire to vote against you. You know this only too well; 'tis for this you rock him to sleep with your lies.

CLEON
Is it not shameful, that you should dare thus to calumniate me before Demos, me, to whom Athens, I swear it by Demeter, already owes more than it ever did to Themistocles?

SAUSAGE-SELLER
Oh! citizens of Argos, do you hear what he says? You dare to compare yourself to Themistocles, who found our city half empty and left it full to overflowing, who one day gave us the Piraeus for dinner, and added fresh fish to all our usual meals. You, on the contrary, you, who compare yourself with

Themistocles, have only sought to reduce our city in size, to shut it within its walls, to chant oracles to us. And Themistocles goes into exile, while you gorge yourself on the most excellent fare.

CLEON
Oh! Demos! Am I compelled to hear myself thus abused, and merely because I love you?

DEMOS
Silence! stop your abuse! All too long have I been your tool.

SAUSAGE-SELLER
Ah! my dear little Demos, he is a rogue, who has played you many a scurvy trick; when your back is turned, he taps at the root the lawsuits initiated by the peculators, swallows the proceeds wholesale and helps himself with both hands from the public funds.

CLEON
Tremble, knave; I will convict you of having stolen thirty thousand drachmae.

SAUSAGE-SELLER
For a rascal of your kidney, you shout rarely! Well! I am ready to die if I do not prove that you have accepted more than forty minae from the Mitylenaeans.

CHORUS
This indeed may be termed talking. Oh, benefactor of the human race, proceed and you will be the most illustrious of the Greeks. You alone shall have sway in Athens, the allies will obey you, and, trident in hand, you will go about shaking and overturning everything to enrich yourself. But, stick to your man, let him not go; with lungs like yours you will soon have him finished.

CLEON
No, my brave friends, no, you are running too fast; I have done a sufficiently brilliant deed to shut the mouth of all enemies, so long as one of the bucklers of Pylos remains.

SAUSAGE-SELLER
Of the bucklers! Hold! I stop you there and I hold you fast. For if it be true, that you love the people, you would not allow these to be hung up with their rings; but 'tis with an intent you have done this. Demos, take knowledge of his guilty purpose; in this way you no longer can punish him at your pleasure. Note the swarm of young tanners, who really surround him, and close to them the sellers of honey and cheese; all these are at one with him. Very well! you have but to frown, to speak of ostracism and they will rush at night to these bucklers, take them down and seize our granaries.

DEMOS
Great gods! what! the bucklers retain their rings! Scoundrel! ah! too long have you had me for your tool, cheated and played with me!

CLEON
But, dear sir, never you believe all he tells you. Oh! never will you find a more devoted friend than me; unaided, I have known how to put down the conspiracies; nothing that is a-hatching in the city escapes me, and I hasten to proclaim it loudly.

SAUSAGE-SELLER
You are like the fishers for eels; in still waters they catch nothing, but if they thoroughly stir up the slime, their fishing is good; in the same way 'tis only in troublous times that you line your pockets.

But come, tell me, you, who sell so many skins, have you ever made him a present of a pair of soles for his slippers? and you pretend to love him!

DEMOS
No, he has never given me any.

SAUSAGE-SELLER
That alone shows up the man; but I, I have bought you this pair of shoes; accept them.

DEMOS
None ever, to my knowledge, has merited so much from the people; you are the most zealous of all men for your country and for my toes.

CLEON
Can a wretched pair of slippers make you forget all that you owe me? Is it not I who curbed Gryttus, the filthiest of the lewd, by depriving him of his citizen rights?

SAUSAGE-SELLER
Ah! noble inspector of back passages, let me congratulate you. Moreover, if you set yourself against this form of lewdness, this pederasty, 'twas for sheer jealousy, knowing it to be the school for orators. But you see this poor Demos without a cloak and that at his age too! so little do you care for him, that in mid-winter you have not given him a garment with sleeves. Here, Demos, here is one, take it!

DEMOS
This even Themistocles never thought of; the Piraeus was no doubt a happy idea, but meseems this tunic is quite as fine an invention.

CLEON
Must you have recourse to such jackanapes' tricks to supplant me?

SAUSAGE-SELLER
No, 'tis your own tricks that I am borrowing, just as a guest, driven by urgent need, seizes some other man's shoes.

CLEON
Oh! you shall not outdo me in flattery! I am going to hand Demos this garment; all that remains to you, you rogue, is to go and hang yourself.

DEMOS
Faugh! may the plague seize you! You stink of leather horribly.

SAUSAGE-SELLER
Why, 'tis to smother you that he has thrown this cloak around you on top of the other; and it is not the first plot he has planned against you. Do you remember the time when silphium was so cheap?

DEMOS
Aye, to be sure I do!

SAUSAGE-SELLER

Very well! it was Cleon who had caused the price to fall so low so that all could eat it and the jurymen in the Courts were almost poisoned with farting in each others' faces.

DEMOS
Hah! why, indeed, a scavenger told me the same thing.

SAUSAGE-SELLER
Were you not yourself in those days quite red in the gills with farting?

DEMOS
Why, 'twas a trick worthy of Pyrrandrus!

CLEON
With what other idle trash will you seek to ruin me, you wretch!

SAUSAGE-SELLER
Oh! I shall be more brazen than you, for 'tis the goddess who has commanded me.

CLEON
No, on my honour, you will not! Here, Demos, feast on this dish; it is your salary as a dicast, which you gain through me for doing naught.

SAUSAGE-SELLER
Hold! here is a little box of ointment to rub into the sores on your legs.

CLEON
I will pluck out your white hairs and make you young again.

SAUSAGE-SELLER
Take this hare's scut to wipe the rheum from your eyes.

CLEON
When you wipe your nose, clean your fingers on my head.

SAUSAGE-SELLER
No, on mine.

CLEON
On mine. [To the **SAUSAGE-SELLER**] I will have you made a trierarch and you will get ruined through it; I will arrange that you are given an old vessel with rotten sails, which you will have to repair constantly and at great cost.

CHORUS
Our man is on the boil; enough, enough, he is boiling over; remove some of the embers from under him and skim off his threats.

CLEON
I will punish your self-importance; I will crush you with imposts; I will have you inscribed on the list of the rich.

SAUSAGE-SELLER

For me no threats—only one simple wish. That you may be having some cuttle-fish fried on the stove just as you are going to set forth to plead the cause of the Milesians, which, if you gain, means a talent in your pocket; that you hurry over devouring the fish to rush off to the Assembly; suddenly you are called and run off with your mouth full so as not to lose the talent and choke yourself. There! that is my wish.

CHORUS
Splendid! by Zeus, Apollo and Demeter!

DEMOS
Faith! here is an excellent citizen indeed, such as has not been seen for a long time. 'Tis truly a man of the lowest scum! As for you, Paphlagonian, who pretend to love me, you only feed me on garlic. Return me my ring, for you cease to be my steward.

CLEON
Here it is, but be assured, that if you bereave me of my power, my successor will be worse than I am.

DEMOS
This cannot be my ring; I see another device, unless I am going purblind.

SAUSAGE-SELLER
What was your device?

DEMOS
A fig-leaf, stuffed with bullock's fat.

SAUSAGE-SELLER
No, that is not it.

DEMOS
What is it then?

SAUSAGE-SELLER
'Tis a gull with beak wide open, haranguing from the top of a stone.

DEMOS
Ah! great gods!

SAUSAGE-SELLER
What is the matter?

DEMOS
Away! away out of my sight! 'Tis not my ring he had, 'twas that of Cleonymus. [To the **SAUSAGE-SELLER**] Hold, I give you this one; you shall be my steward.

CLEON
Master, I adjure you, decide nothing till you have heard my oracles.

SAUSAGE-SELLER
And mine.

CLEON
If you believe him, you will have to suck his tool for him.

SAUSAGE-SELLER
If you listen to him, you'll have to let him skin your penis to the very stump.

CLEON
My oracles say that you are to reign over the whole earth, crowned with chaplets.

SAUSAGE-SELLER
And mine say that, clothed in an embroidered purple robe, you shall pursue Smicythes and her spouse, standing in a chariot of gold and with a crown on your head.

DEMOS
Go, fetch me your oracles, that the Paphlagonian may hear them.

SAUSAGE-SELLER
Willingly.

DEMOS
And you yours.

CLEON
I run.

SAUSAGE-SELLER
And I run too; nothing could suit me better!

CHORUS
Oh! happy day for us and for our children, if Cleon perish. Yet just now I heard some old cross-grained pleaders on the market-place who hold not this opinion discoursing together. Said they, "If Cleon had not had the power we should have lacked two most useful tools, the pestle and the soup-ladle." You also know what a pig's education he has had; his school-fellows can recall that he only liked the Dorian style and would study no other; his music-master in displeasure sent him away, saying: "This youth in matters of harmony, will only learn the Dorian style because 'tis akin to bribery."

CLEON
There, behold and look at this heap; and yet I do not bring all.

SAUSAGE-SELLER
Ugh! I pant and puff under the weight and yet I do not bring all.

DEMOS
What are these?

CLEON
Oracles.

DEMOS
All these?

CLEON
Does that astonish you? Why, I have another whole boxful of them.

SAUSAGE-SELLER
And I the whole of my attics and two rooms besides.

DEMOS
Come, let us see, whose are these oracles?

CLEON
Mine are those of Bacis.

DEMOS [To the **SAUSAGE-SELLER**]
And whose are yours?

SAUSAGE-SELLER
Glanis's, the elder brother of Bacis.

DEMOS
And of what do they speak?

CLEON
Of Athens, of Pylos, of you, of me, of all.

DEMOS
And yours?

SAUSAGE-SELLER
Of Athens, of lentils, of Lacedaemonians, of fresh mackerel, of scoundrelly flour-sellers, of you, of me. Ah! ha! now let him gnaw his own penis with chagrin!

DEMOS
Come, read them out to me and especially that one I like so much, which says that I shall become an eagle and soar among the clouds.

CLEON
Then listen and be attentive! "Son of Erectheus, understand the meaning of the words, which the sacred tripods set resounding in the sanctuary of Apollo. Preserve the sacred dog with the jagged teeth, that barks and howls in your defence; he will ensure you a salary and, if he fails, will perish as the victim of the swarms of jays that hunt him down with their screams."

DEMOS
By Demeter! I do not understand a word of it. What connection is there between Erectheus, the jays and the dog?

CLEON
'Tis I who am the dog, since I bark in your defence. Well! Phoebus commands you to keep and cherish your dog.

SAUSAGE-SELLER

'Tis not so spoken by the god; this dog seems to me to gnaw at the oracles as others gnaw at doorposts. Here is exactly what Apollo says of the dog.

DEMOS
Let us hear, but I must first pick up a stone; an oracle which speaks of a dog might bite me.

SAUSAGE-SELLER
"Son of Erectheus, beware of this Cerberus that enslaves freemen; he fawns upon you with his tail, when you are dining, but he is lying in wait to devour your dishes, should you turn your head an instant; at night he sneaks into the kitchen and, true dog that he is, licks up with one lap of his tongue both your dishes and ... the islands."

DEMOS
Faith, Glanis, you speak better than your brother.

CLEON
Condescend again to hear me and then judge: "A woman in sacred Athens will be delivered of a lion, who shall fight for the people against clouds of gnats with the same ferocity as if he were defending his whelps; care ye for him, erect wooden walls around him and towers of brass." Do you understand that?

DEMOS
Not the least bit in the world.

CLEON
The god tells you here to look after me, for, 'tis I who am your lion.

DEMOS
How! You have become a lion and I never knew a thing about it?

SAUSAGE-SELLER
There is only one thing which he purposely keeps from you; he does not say what this wall of wood and brass is in which Apollo warns you to keep and guard him.

DEMOS
What does the god mean, then?

SAUSAGE-SELLER
He advises you to fit him into a five-holed wooden collar.

DEMOS
Hah! I think that oracle is about to be fulfilled.

CLEON
Do not believe it; these are but jealous crows, that caw against me; but never cease to cherish your good hawk; never forget that he brought you those Lacedaemonian fish, loaded with chains.

SAUSAGE-SELLER
Ah! if the Paphlagonian ran any risk that day, 'twas because he was drunk. Oh, too credulous son of Cecrops, do you accept that as a glorious exploit? A woman would carry a heavy burden if only a man had put it on her shoulders. But to fight! Go to! he would shit himself, if ever it came to a tussle.

CLEON
Note this Pylos in front of Pylos, of which the oracle speaks, "Pylos is before Pylos."

DEMOS
How "in front of Pylos"? What does he mean by that?

SAUSAGE-SELLER
He says he will seize upon your bath-tubs.

DEMOS
Then I shall not bathe to-day.

SAUSAGE-SELLER
No, as he has stolen our baths. But here is an oracle about the fleet, to which I beg your best attention.

DEMOS
Read on! I am listening; let us first see how we are to pay our sailors.

SAUSAGE-SELLER
"Son of Aegeus, beware of the tricks of the dog-fox, he bites from the rear and rushes off at full speed; he is nothing but cunning and perfidy." Do you know what the oracle intends to say?

DEMOS
The dog-fox is Philostratus.

SAUSAGE-SELLER
No, no, 'tis Cleon; he is incessantly asking you for light vessels to go and collect the tributes, and Apollo advises you not to grant them.

DEMOS
What connection is there between a galley and a dog-fox?

SAUSAGE-SELLER
What connection? Why, 'tis quite plain—a galley travels as fast as a dog.

DEMOS
Why, then, does the oracle not say dog instead of dog-fox?

SAUSAGE-SELLER
Because he compares the soldiers to young foxes, who, like them, eat the grapes in the fields.

DEMOS
Good! Well then! how am I to pay the wages of my young foxes?

SAUSAGE-SELLER
I will undertake that, and in three days too! But listen to this further oracle, by which Apollo puts you on your guard against the snares of the greedy fist.

DEMOS

Of what greedy fist?

SAUSAGE-SELLER
The god in this oracle very clearly points to the hand of Cleon, who incessantly holds his out, saying, "Fill it."

CLEON
'Tis false! Phoebus means the hand of Diopithes. But here I have a winged oracle, which promises you shall become an eagle and rule over all the earth.

SAUSAGE-SELLER
I have one, which says that you shall be King of the Earth and of the Sea, and that you shall administer justice in Ecbatana, eating fine rich stews the while.

CLEON
I have seen Athené in a dream, pouring out full vials of riches and health over the people.

SAUSAGE-SELLER
I too have seen the goddess, descending from the Acropolis with an owl perched upon her helmet; on your head she was pouring out ambrosia, on that of Cleon garlic pickle.

DEMOS
Truly Glanis is the wisest of men. I shall yield myself to you; guide me in my old age and educate me anew.

CLEON
Ah! I adjure you! not yet; wait a little; I will promise to distribute barley every day.

DEMOS
Ah! I will not hear another word about barley; you have cheated me too often already, both you and Theophanes.

CLEON
Well then! you shall have flour-cakes all piping hot.

SAUSAGE-SELLER
I will give you cakes too, and nice cooked fish; you will only have to eat.

DEMOS
Very well, mind you keep your promises. To whichever of you twain shall treat me best I hand over the reins of state.

CLEON
I will be first.

SAUSAGE-SELLER
No, no, I will.

CHORUS

Demos, you are our all-powerful sovereign lord; all tremble before you, yet you are led by the nose. You love to be flattered and fooled; you listen to the orators with gaping mouth and your mind is led astray.

DEMOS
'Tis rather you who have no brains, if you think me so foolish as all that; it is with a purpose that I play this idiot's role, for I love to drink the lifelong day, and so it pleases me to keep a thief for my minister. When he has thoroughly gorged himself, then I overthrow and crush him.

CHORUS
What profound wisdom! If it be really so, why! all is for the best. Your ministers, then, are your victims, whom you nourish and feed up expressly in the Pnyx, so that, the day your dinner is ready, you may immolate the fattest and eat him.

DEMOS
Look, see how I play with them, while all the time they think themselves such adepts at cheating me. I have my eye on them when they thieve, but I do not appear to be seeing them; then I thrust a judgment down their throat as it were a feather, and force them to vomit up all they have robbed from me.

CLEON
Oh! the rascal!

SAUSAGE-SELLER
Oh! the scoundrel!

CLEON
Demos, all is ready these three hours; I await your orders and I burn with desire to load you with benefits.

SAUSAGE-SELLER
And I ten, twelve, a thousand hours, a long, long while, an infinitely long while.

DEMOS
As for me, 'tis thirty thousand hours that I have been impatient; very long, infinitely long that I have cursed you.

SAUSAGE SELLER
Do you know what you had best do?

DEMOS
If I do not, tell me.

SAUSAGE-SELLER
Declare the lists open and we will contend abreast to determine who shall treat you the best.

DEMOS
Splendid! Draw back in line!

CLEON
I am ready.

DEMOS
Off you go!

SAUSAGE-SELLER [To **CLEON**]
I shall not let you get to the tape.

DEMOS
What fervent lovers! If I am not to-day the happiest of men, 'tis because I shall be the most disgusted.

CLEON
Look! 'tis I who am the first to bring you a seat.

SAUSAGE-SELLER
And I a table.

CLEON
Hold, here is a cake kneaded of Pylos barley.

SAUSAGE-SELLER
Here are crusts, which the ivory hand of the goddess has hallowed.

DEMOS
Oh! Mighty Athené! How large are your fingers!

CLEON
This is pea-soup, as exquisite as it is fine; 'tis Pallas the victorious goddess at Pylos who crushed the peas herself.

SAUSAGE-SELLER
Oh, Demos! the goddess watches over you; she is stretching forth over your head ... a stew-pan full of broth.

DEMOS
And should we still be dwelling in this city without this protecting stew-pan?

CLEON
Here are some fish, given to you by her who is the terror of our foes.

SAUSAGE-SELLER
The daughter of the mightiest of the gods sends you this meat cooked in its own gravy, along with this dish of tripe and some paunch.

DEMOS
'Tis to thank me for the Peplos I offered to her; 'tis well.

CLEON
The goddess with the terrible plume invites you to eat this long cake; you will row the harder on it.

SAUSAGE-SELLER

Take this also.

DEMOS
And what shall I do with this tripe?

SAUSAGE-SELLER
She sends it you to belly out your galleys, for she is always showing her kindly anxiety for our fleet. Now drink this beverage composed of three parts of water to two of wine.

DEMOS
Ah! what delicious wine, and how well it stands the water.

SAUSAGE-SELLER
'Twas the goddess who came from the head of Zeus that mixed this liquor with her own hands.

CLEON
Hold, here is a piece of good rich cake.

SAUSAGE-SELLER
But I offer you an entire cake.

CLEON
But you cannot offer him stewed hare as I do.

SAUSAGE-SELLER
Ah! great gods! stewed hare! where shall I find it? Oh! brain of mine, devise some trick!

CLEON
Do you see this, poor fellow?

SAUSAGE-SELLER
A fig for that! Here are folk coming to seek me.

CLEON
Who are they?

SAUSAGE-SELLER
Envoys, bearing sacks bulging with money.

CLEON [Hearing money mentioned **CLEON** turns his head, and **AGORACRITUS** seizes the opportunity to snatch away the stewed hare.]
Where, where, I say?

SAUSAGE-SELLER
Bah! What's that to you? Will you not even now let the strangers alone? Demos, do you see this stewed hare which I bring you?

CLEON
Ah! rascal! you have shamelessly robbed me.

SAUSAGE-SELLER

You have robbed too, you robbed the Laconians at Pylos.

DEMOS
An you pity me, tell me, how did you get the idea to filch it from him?

SAUSAGE-SELLER
The idea comes from the goddess; the theft is all my own.

CLEON
And I had taken such trouble to catch this hare.

SAUSAGE-SELLER
But 'twas I who had it cooked.

DEMOS [To **CLEON**]
Get you gone! My thanks are only for him who served it.

CLEON
Ah! wretch! have you beaten me in impudence!

SAUSAGE-SELLER
Well then, Demos, say now, who has treated you best, you and your stomach? Decide!

DEMOS
How shall I act here so that the spectators shall approve my judgment?

SAUSAGE-SELLER
I will tell you. Without saying anything, go and rummage through my basket, and then through the Paphlagonian's, and see what is in them; that's the best way to judge.

DEMOS
Let us see then, what is there in yours?

SAUSAGE-SELLER
Why, 'tis empty, dear little father; I have brought everything to you.

DEMOS
This is a basket devoted to the people.

SAUSAGE-SELLER
Now hunt through the Paphlagonian's. Well?

DEMOS
Oh! what a lot of good things! Why! 'tis quite full! Oh! what a huge great part of this cake he kept for himself! He had only cut off the least little tiny piece for me.

SAUSAGE-SELLER
But this is what he has always done. Of everything he took, he only gave you the crumbs, and kept the bulk.

DEMOS

Oh! rascal! was this the way you robbed me? And I was loading you with chaplets and gifts!

CLEON
'Twas for the public weal I robbed.

DEMOS [To **CLEON**]
Give me back that crown; I will give it to him.

SAUSAGE-SELLER
Return it quick, quick, you gallows-bird.

CLEON
No, for the Pythian oracle has revealed to me the name of him who shall overthrow me.

SAUSAGE-SELLER
And that name was mine, nothing can be clearer.

CLEON
Reply and I shall soon see whether you are indeed the man whom the god intended. Firstly, what school did you attend when a child?

SAUSAGE-SELLER
'Twas in the kitchens I was taught with cuffs and blows.

CLEON
What's that you say? Ah! this is truly what the oracle said. And what did you learn from the master of exercises?

SAUSAGE-SELLER
I learnt to take a false oath without a smile, when I had stolen something.

CLEON
Oh! Phoebus Apollo, god of Lycia! I am undone! And when you had become a man, what trade did you follow?

SAUSAGE-SELLER
I sold sausages and did a bit of fornication.

CLEON
Oh! my god! I am a lost man! Ah! still one slender hope remains. Tell me, was it on the market-place or near the gates that you sold your sausages?

SAUSAGE-SELLER
Near the gates, in the market for salted goods.

CLEON
Alas! I see the prophecy of the god is verily come true. Alas! Roll me home. I am a miserable, ruined man. Farewell, my chaplet! 'Tis death to me to part with you. So you are to belong to another; 'tis certain he cannot be a greater thief, but perhaps he may be a luckier one.

SAUSAGE-SELLER

Oh! Zeus, the protector of Greece! 'tis to you I owe this victory!

DEMOSTHENES
Hail! illustrious conqueror, but forget not, that if you have become a great man, 'tis thanks to me; I ask but a little thing; appoint me secretary of the law-court in the room of Phanus.

DEMOS [To the **SAUSAGE-SELLER**]
But what is your name then? Tell me.

SAUSAGE-SELLER
My name is Agoracritus, because I have always lived on the market-place in the midst of lawsuits.

DEMOS
Well then, Agoracritus, I stand by you; as for the Paphlagonian, I hand him over to your mercy.

AGORACRITUS
Demos, I will care for you to the best of my power, and all shall admit that no citizen is more devoted than I to this city of simpletons.

CHORUS
What fitter theme for our Muse, at the close as at the beginning of his work, than this, to sing the hero who drives his swift steeds down the arena? Why afflict Lysistratus with our satires on his poverty, and Thumantis, who has not so much as a lodging? He is dying of hunger and can be seen at Delphi, his face bathed in tears, clinging to your quiver, oh, Apollo! and supplicating you to take him out of his misery.

An insult directed at the wicked is not to be censured; on the contrary, the honest man, if he has sense, can only applaud. Him, whom I wish to brand with infamy, is little known himself; 'tis the brother of Arignotus. I regret to quote this name which is so dear to me, but whoever can distinguish black from white, or the Orthian mode of music from others, knows the virtues of Arignotus, whom his brother, Ariphrades, in no way resembles. He gloats in vice, is not merely a dissolute man and utterly debauched—but he has actually invented a new form of vice; for he pollutes his tongue with abominable pleasures in brothels licking up that nauseous moisture and befouling his beard as he tickles the lips of lewd women's private parts. Whoever is not horrified at such a monster shall never drink from the same cup with me.

At times a thought weighs on me at night; I wonder whence comes this fearful voracity of Cleonymus. 'Tis said, that when dining with a rich host, he springs at the dishes with the gluttony of a wild beast and never leaves the bread-bin until his host seizes him round the knees, exclaiming, "Go, go, good gentleman, in mercy go, and spare my poor table!"

'Tis said that the triremes assembled in council and that the oldest spoke in these terms, "Are you ignorant, my sisters, of what is plotting in Athens? They say, that a certain Hyperbolus, a bad citizen and an infamous scoundrel, asks for a hundred of us to take them to sea against Chalcedon." All were indignant, and one of them, as yet a virgin, cried, "May god forbid that I should ever obey him! I would prefer to grow old in the harbour and be gnawed by worms. No! by the gods I swear it, Nauphanté, daughter of Nauson, shall never bend to his law; 'tis as true as I am made of wood and pitch. If the Athenians vote for the proposal of Hyperbolus, let them! we will hoist full sail and seek refuge by the temple of Theseus or the shrine of the Euminides. No! he shall not command us! No! he shall not play with the city to this extent! Let him sail by himself for Tartarus, if such please him, launching the boats in which he used to sell his lamps."

AGORACRITUS
Maintain a holy silence! Keep your mouths from utterance! call no more witnesses; close these tribunals, which are the delight of this city, and gather at the theatre to chant the Paean of thanksgiving to the gods for a fresh favour.

CHORUS
Oh! torch of sacred Athens, saviour of the Islands, what good tidings are we to celebrate by letting the blood of the victims flow in our market-places?

AGORACRITUS
I have freshened Demos up somewhat on the stove and have turned his ugliness into beauty.

CHORUS
I admire your inventive genius; but, where is he?

AGORACRITUS
He is living in ancient Athens, the city of the garlands of violets.

CHORUS
How I should like to see him! What is his dress like, what his manner?

AGORACRITUS
He has once more become as he was in the days when he lived with Aristides and Miltiades. But you will judge for yourselves, for I hear the vestibule doors opening. Hail with your shouts of gladness the Athens of old, which now doth reappear to your gaze, admirable, worthy of the songs of the poets and the home of the illustrious Demos.

CHORUS
Oh! noble, brilliant Athens, whose brow is wreathed with violets, show us the sovereign master of this land and of all Greece.

AGORACRITUS
Lo! here he is coming with his hair held in place with a golden band and in all the glory of his old-world dress; perfumed with myrrh, he spreads around him not the odour of lawsuits, but of peace.

CHORUS
Hail! King of Greece, we congratulate you upon the happiness you enjoy; it is worthy of this city, worthy of the glory of Marathon.

DEMOS
Come, Agoracritus, come, my best friend; see the service you have done me by freshening me up on your stove.

AGORACRITUS
Ah! if you but remembered what you were formerly and what you did, you would for a certainty believe me to be a god.

DEMOS
But what did I? and how was I then?

AGORACRITUS
Firstly, so soon as ever an orator declared in the assembly "Demos, I love you ardently; 'tis I alone, who dream of you and watch over your interests"; at such an exordium you would look like a cock flapping his wings or a bull tossing his horns.

DEMOS
What, I?

AGORACRITUS
Then, after he had fooled you to the hilt, he would go.

DEMOS
What! they would treat me so, and I never saw it!

AGORACRITUS
You knew only how to open and close your ears like a sunshade.

DEMOS
Was I then so stupid and such a dotard?

AGORACRITUS
Worse than that; if one of two orators proposed to equip a fleet for war and the other suggested the use of the same sum for paying out to the citizens, 'twas the latter who always carried the day. Well! you droop your head! you turn away your face?

DEMOS
I redden at my past errors.

AGORACRITUS
Think no more of them; 'tis not you who are to blame, but those who cheated you in this sorry fashion. But, come, if some impudent lawyer dared to say, "Dicasts, you shall have no wheat unless you convict this accused man!" what would you do? Tell me.

DEMOS
I would have him removed from the bar, I would bind Hyperbolus about his neck like a stone and would fling him into the Barathrum.

AGORACRITUS
Well spoken! but what other measures do you wish to take?

DEMOS
First, as soon as ever a fleet returns to the harbour, I shall pay up the rowers in full.

AGORACRITUS
That will soothe many a worn and chafed bottom.

DEMOS
Further, the hoplite enrolled for military service shall not get transferred to another service through favour, but shall stick to that given him at the outset.

AGORACRITUS

This will strike the buckler of Cleonymus full in the centre.

DEMOS
None shall ascend the rostrum, unless their chins are bearded.

AGORACRITUS
What then will become of Clisthenes and of Strato?

DEMOS
I wish only to refer to those youths, who loll about the perfume shops, babbling at random, "What a clever fellow is Pheax! How cleverly he escaped death! how concise and convincing is his style! what phrases! how clear and to the point! how well he knows how to quell an interruption!"

AGORACRITUS
I thought you were the lover of those pathic minions.

DEMOS
The gods forefend it! and I will force all such fellows to go a-hunting instead of proposing decrees.

AGORACRITUS
In that case, accept this folding-stool, and to carry it this well-grown, big-testicled slave lad. Besides, you may put him to any other purpose you please.

DEMOS
Oh! I am happy indeed to find myself as I was of old!

AGORACRITUS
Aye, you deem yourself happy, when I shall have handed you the truces of thirty years. Truces! step forward!

DEMOS
Great gods! how charming they are! Can I do with them as I wish? where did you discover them, pray?

AGORACRITUS
'Twas that Paphlagonian who kept them locked up in his house, so that you might not enjoy them. As for myself, I give them to you; take them with you into the country.

DEMOS
And what punishment will you inflict upon this Paphlagonian, the cause of all my troubles?

AGORACRITUS
'Twill not be over-terrible. I condemn him to follow my old trade; posted near the gates, he must sell sausages of asses' and dogs'-meat; perpetually drunk, he will exchange foul language with prostitutes and will drink nothing but the dirty water from the baths.

DEMOS
Well conceived! he is indeed fit to wrangle with harlots and bathmen; as for you, in return for so many blessings, I invite you to take the place at the Prytaneum which this rogue once occupied. Put on this frog-green mantle and follow me. As for the other, let 'em take him away; let him go sell his sausages in full view of the foreigners, whom he used formerly so wantonly to insult.

Aristophanes – A Short Biography

Of Aristophanes, the greatest comedian of his age, and perhaps of all the ages, history contains few notices, and these of doubtful credit. Even the dates of his birth and death can only be inferred from his works, the former being estimated at 456 B.C. and the latter at 380. Many cities claimed the honor of giving him birth, the most probable story making him the son of Philippus of Ægina, and therefore only an adopted citizen of Athens. On this point some confusion has arisen from an attempt of Cleon to deprive Aristophanes of his civic rights, on the ground of illegitimacy, in revenge for his frequent invectives. The charge was disproved, thus pointing to the Athenian parentage of the comic poet, though as to this there is no trustworthy evidence. He was doubtless educated at Athens, and among other advantages is said to have been a disciple of Prodicus, though in his mention of that sophist he shows none of the respect due to his reputed master.

It was under the mighty genius of Aristophanes that the old Attic comedy received its fullest development. Dignified by the acquisition of a chorus of masked actors, and of scenery and machinery, and by a corresponding literary elaboration and elegance of style, comedy nevertheless remained true both to its origin and to the purposes of its introduction into the free imperial city. It borrowed much from tragedy, but it retained the Phallic abandonment of the old rural festivals, the license of word and gesture, and the audacious directness of personal invective. These characteristics are not features peculiar to Aristophanes. He was twitted by some of the older comic poets with having degenerated from the full freedom of the art through a tendency to refinement, and he took credit to himself for having superseded the time-honored can can and the stale practical joking of his predecessors by a nobler kind of mirth. But in boldness, as he likewise boasted, he had no peer; and the shafts of his wit, though dipped in wine-lees and at times feathered from very obscene fowl, flew at high game. He has been accused of seeking to degrade what he ought to have recognized as good; and it has been shown by competent critics that he is not to be taken as an impartial or accurate authority on Athenian history. But, partisan as he was, he was also a genuine patriot, and his very political sympathies—which were conservative—were such as have often stimulated the most effective political satire, because they imply an antipathy to every species of excess. Of reverence he was, however, altogether devoid; and his love for Athens was that of the most free-spoken of sons. Flexible, even in his religious notions, he was in this, as in other respects, ready to be educated by his times; and, like a true comic poet, he could be witty at the expense even of his friends, and, it might almost be said, of himself. In wealth of fancy and in beauty of lyric melody he ranks high among the great poets of all times.

It has been said that Aristophanes was an unmannerly buffoon, and so, indeed, he was, among his other faults. Nor was he at all justified in stooping to this degradation, whether it were that he was instigated by coarse inclinations, or that he held it necessary to gain over the populace, that he might have it in his power to tell such bold truths to the people. At least he makes it his boast that he did not court the laughter of the multitude so much as his rivals did, by mere indecent buffoonery, and that in this respect he brought his art to perfection. Not to be unreasonable, we should judge him from the standpoint of his own times, in respect of those peculiarities which make him offensive to us. On certain points, the ancients had quite a different morality from ours, and certainly a much freer one. This arose from their religion, which was a real worship of Nature, and had given sanctity to many public ceremonies which grossly violate decency. Moreover, as in consequence of the seclusion of their women, the men were almost always together, a certain coarseness entered into their conversation, as in such circumstances is apt to be the case.

The strongest testimony in favor of Aristophanes is that of Plato, who, in one of his epigrams, says that "the Graces chose his soul for their abode." The philosopher was a constant reader of the comedian, sending to Dionysius the elder a copy of the Clouds, from which to make himself acquainted with the Athenian republic. This was not intended merely as a description of the unbridled democratic freedom then prevailing at Athens, but as an example of the poet's thorough knowledge of the world, and of the political conditions of what was then the world's metropolis.

In his Symposium, Plato makes Aristophanes deliver a discourse on love, which the latter explains in a sensual manner, but with remarkable originality. At the end of the banquet, Aristodemus, who was one of the guests, fell asleep, "and, as the nights were long, took a good rest. When he was awakened, toward daybreak, by the crowing of cocks, the others were also asleep or had gone away, and there remained awake only Aristophanes, Agathon and Socrates, who were drinking out of a large goblet that was passed around, while Socrates was discoursing to them. Aristodemus did not hear all the discourse, for he was only half awake; but he remembered Socrates insisting to the other two that the genius of comedy was the same as that of tragedy, and that the writer of the one should also be a writer of the other. To this they were compelled to assent, being sleepy, and not quite understanding what he meant. And first Aristophanes fell asleep, and then, when the day was dawning, Agathon."

The words applied by Goethe to a shrewd adventurer, "mad, but clever," might also be used of the plays of Aristophanes, which are the very intoxication of poetry, the Bacchanalia of mirth. For mirth will maintain its rights as well as the other faculties; therefore, different nations have set apart certain holidays for jovial folly, and such as their saturnalia, their carnival, that being once satisfied to their hearts' content, they might keep themselves sober all the rest of the year, and leave free room for serious occupation. The old comedy is a general masquerade of the world, beneath which there passes much that is not allowed by the common rules of propriety; but at the same time much that is amusing, clever, and even instructive is brought to light, which would not have been possible but for the demolition for the moment of these barricades.

However corrupt and vulgar Aristophanes may have been in his personal propensities, however much he may offend decency and taste in his individual jests, yet in the plan and conduct of his poems in general, we cannot refuse him the praise of the carefulness and masterly skill of the finished artist. His language is infinitely graceful; the purest Atticism prevails in it, and he adapts it with great skill to all tones, from the most familiar dialogue to the lofty flight of the dithyrambic ode. We cannot doubt that he would have also succeeded in more serious poetry, when we see how at times he lavishes it, merely to annihilate its impression immediately afterward. This elegance is rendered the more attractive by contrast, since on the one hand he admist the rudest expressions of the people, the dialects, and even the mutilated Greek of barbarians, while on the other, the same arbitrary caprice which he brought to his views of universal nature and the human world, he also applies to language, and by composition, by allusion and personal names, or imitation of sound, forms the strangest words imaginable. His versification is not less artificial than that of the tragedians; he uses the same forms, but otherwise modified, as his personages are not to be impressive and dignified, but of a light and varied character; yet with all this seeming irregularity he observes the laws of metre no less strictly than the tragic poets do.

As we cannot help recognizing in Aristophanes' exercise of his varied and multiform art, the richest development of almost every poetical talent, so the extraordinary capacities of his hearers, which may be inferred from the structure of his works, are at every fresh perusal a matter of astonishment. Accurate acquaintance with the history and constitution of their country, with public events and proceedings, with the personal circumstances of almost all remarkable contemporaries, might be expected from the citizens of a democratic republic. But, besides this, Aristophanes required from his audience much poetic culture; especially they had to retain in their memories the tragic masterpieces, almost word by word, in order to understand his parodies.

The old comedy of the Greeks would have been impossible under any other form of government than a complete and unrestricted democracy; for it exercised a satirical censorship unsparing of public and private life, of statesmanship, of political and social usage, of education and literature, in a word, of everything which concerned the city, or could amuse the citizens. Retaining all the license, the riot and exuberance which marked its origin, it combined with this an expression of public opinion in such form that neither vice, misconduct, nor folly could venture to disregard it. If it was disfigured by grossness and licentiousness, this, it must be remembered, was in keeping with the sentiment of Dionysian festivals, just as a decorous cheerfulness was expected at festivals in honor of Apollo or Athena. To omit these features from comedy would be to deprive it of its most popular element, and without them the entertainment would have fallen flat.

Greek literature was immeasurably rich in this department: the names of the lost comedians, most of whom were very prolific, and of their works, so far as we are acquainted with them, would alone form a bulky catalogue. Although the new comedy unfolded itself, and flourished only for some eighty years, the number of plays certainly amounted to a thousand at least; but time has made such havoc with this superabundance of works that nothing remains except detached fragments in the original language, in many cases so disfigured as to be unintelligible, and in the Latin, a number of translations or adaptations of Greek originals.

For a comic poet who was unquestionably at the head of the fraternity, and in sentiment was intensely patriotic, the consciousness of his recognized power and the desire to use it for the good of his native city must ever have been the prevailing motives. At Athens such a man held an influence resembling rather that of the modern journalist than the modern dramatist; but the established type of comedy gave him an instrument such as no public satirist ever wielded, before or since. He was under no such limitations as to form or process, allusion or emphasis, as is the modern dramatist, and could indulge in the wildest flights of extravagance. After his keenest thrust or most passionate appeal, he could at once change his subject from the grave to the burlesque, and, in short, there was no limit to his field for invective and satire.

"Aristophanes," as one of his critics remarks, "is for us, the representative of old comedy." But it is important to notice that his genius, while it includes, also transcends the genius of the old comedy. He can denounce the frauds of Cleon, he can vindicate the duty of Athens to herself and to her allies with a stinging scorn and a force of patriotic indignation which make the poet almost forgotten in the citizen. He can banter Euripides with an ingenuity of light mockery which makes it seem for the time as if the leading Aristophonic trait was the art of seeing all things from their prosaic side. Yet it is neither in the denunciation nor in the mockery that he is most individual. His truest and highest faculty is revealed by those wonderful bits of lyric writing in which he soars above everything that can move laughter or tears, and makes the clear air thrill with the notes of a song as free, as musical and as wild as that of the nightingale invoked by his own chorus in the Birds. The speech of True Logic in the Clouds, the praises of country life in the Peace, the serenade in the Eccleziazusae, the songs of the Spartan and Athenian maidens in the Lysistrata, above all, perhaps the chorus in the Frogs, the beautiful chant of the Initiated—these passages, and such as these, are the true glories of Aristophanes. They are the strains, not of an artist, but of one who warbles for pure gladness of heart in some place made bright by the presence of a god. Nothing else in Greek poetry has quite this wild sweetness of the woods. Of modern poets Shakespeare alone, perhaps, has it in combination with a like richness and fertility of fancy.

A sympathetic reader of Aristophanes can hardly fail to percieve that, while his political and intellectual tendencies are well marked, his opinions, in so far as they color his comedies, are too definite to reward, or indeed to tolerate, analysis. Aristophanes was a natural conservative. His ideal was the Athens of the Persian wars. He disapproved the policy which had made Athenian empire irksome to the allies and formidable to Greece; he detested the vulgarity and the violence of mob-rule; he clave to the old worship of the gods; he regarded the new ideas of education as a tissue of imposture and impiety. How far he was from clearness or precision of view in regard to the intellectual revolution which was going forward appears from the Clouds, in which thinkers and literary workers who had absolutely nothing in common are treated with sweeping ridicule as prophets of a common heresy. Aristophanes is one of the men for whom opinion is mainly a matter of feeling, not of reason. His imaginative susceptibility gave him a warm and loyal love for the traditional glories of Athens, however dim the past to which they belonged; a horror of what was offensive or absurd in pretension. The broad preferences and dislikes thus generated were enough not only to point the moral of comedy, but to make him, in many cases, a really useful censor for the city. The service which he could render in this way was, however, only negative. He could hardly be, in any positive sense, a political or a moral teacher for Athens. His rooted antipathy to intellectual progress, while it affords easy and wide scope for his wit, must, after all, lower his rank. The great minds are not the enemies of ideas. But as a mocker—to use the word which seems most closely to describe him on this side—he is incomparable for the union of subtlety with the riot of comic imagination. As a poet, he is immortal; and, amont Athenian poets, he has for his distinctive characteristic that he is inspired less by that Greek genius which never allows fancy to escape from the control of defining, though spiritualizing reason, than by such ethereal rapture of the unfettered fancy as lifts Shakespeare or Shelley above it,—

"Pouring out his full soul
In profuse strains of unpremeditated art."

Aristophanes – A Concise Bibliography

Surviving Plays

The Acharnians (425 BC)
The Knights (424 BC)
The Clouds (original 423 BC, uncompleted revised version from 419 BC – 416 BC survives)
The Wasps (422 BC)
Peace (first version, 421 BC)
The Birds (414 BC)
Lysistrata (411 BC)
Thesmophoriazusae or The Women Celebrating the Thesmophoria (first version c.411 BC)
The Frogs (405 BC)
Ecclesiazusae or The Assemblywomen; (c. 392 BC)
Wealth (second version, 388 BC)

Dated But Lost Plays

Banqueters (427 BC)
Babylonians (426 BC)
Farmers (424 BC)
Merchant Ships (423 BC)
Clouds (first version) (423 BC)

Proagon (422 BC)
Amphiaraus (A414 BC)
Plutus (first version, 408 BC)
Gerytades (probably 407 BC)
Cocalus (387 BC)
Aiolosicon (second version, 386 BC)

Undated Lost Plays

Aiolosicon (first version)
Anagyrus
Frying-Pan Men
Daedalus
Danaids
Centaur
Heroes
Lemnian Women
Old Age
Peace (second version)
Phoenician Women
Polyidus
Seasons
Storks
Telemessians
Triphales
Thesmophoriazusae (Women at the Thesmophoria Festival, second version)
Women in Tents

www.ingramcontent.com/pod-product-compliance
Lightning Source LLC
LaVergne TN
LVHW012335100826
845148LV00017B/2634

* 9 7 8 1 7 8 7 3 7 1 3 5 4 *